NATIVE
NEW ENGLAND
COOKING

GW00763863

DALE CARSON

PEREGRINE PRESS, Publishers

Old Saybrook, Connecticut

Printing, Inc.
50 Mungertown Road
Madison, CT 0643

Manufactured in the United States of America

Eighth Printing

1993

ISBN 0-933614-05-5

TABLE OF CONTENTS

SEAFOOD

POULTRY AND GAME

VEGETABLES AND SOUPS

BREAD

INTRODUCTION

Everyone knows the story about the starving Pilgrims and the first Thanksgiving, but what most people do not realize is that the Native American of the eastern woodlands was a creative cook long before the white man stepped foot on Plymouth Rock. They had to be. The majority of their food came from the wild, the forest and the sea, and what little cultivating they did was in crops with an incredibly short harvesting season. They had to learn to cook and preserve the summer foods to feed them through the long winters. And they had to devise ways to catch and cook the wild animals and fish that helped sustain them year-round. But despite these problems, they used and blended the things they had and created some wonderful dishes.

With the coming of the first white

3

SETTLERS, INDIAN COOKING BECAME
EVEN MORE WONDERFUL AND VARIED.
THE INDIANS INTRODUCED THE WHITE
MAN TO THEIR THREE MAJOR CROPS:
CORN, BEANS AND SQUASH, WHILE THE
SETTLERS SHOWED THE INDIANS APPLES,
PIGS, COWS AND MOLASSES AMONG OTHER
THINGS. ALSO, THE SETTLERS BROUGHT
IRON POTS WITH THEM, FREEING THE
INDIAN FROM USING HOLLOWED OUT BIRCH
LOGS, AND THEREBY GREATLY EXTENDING
THEIR NATURAL COOKING ABILITY. THE
CULINARY MELDING OF THESE TWO CULTURES
PRODUCED SOME UNUSUAL AND DELICIOUS
RECIPES, SOME OF THE BEST INCLUDED IN
THIS BOOK.

BECAUSE COOKBOOKS WERE VIRTUALLY
UNKNOWN IN THOSE EARLY DAYS, FAVORITE
RECIPES WERE PASSED BY WORD OF MOUTH—
FRIEND TO FRIEND, MOTHER TO DAUGHTER.
MY OWN MOTHER NUTURED MY INTEREST
IN COOKING AND MY INDIAN HERITAGE AND
MANY OF THE FOLLOWING RECIPES CAME
FROM HER.

THIS BOOK IS FOR THOSE WHO ARE NOT

ONLY INTERESTED IN EARLY AMERICAN COOKING, BUT ALSO FOR THOSE WHO SEEK TO FIND SOMETHING PERHAPS A LITTLE DIFFERENT, SOMETHING WHICH SPRINGS FROM THE VERY BEGINNINGS OF OUR CULTURE BUT WHICH ALSO TASTES DARN GOOD. ALL OF THE SAME BASIC FOODS THAT WERE HERE IN THOSE EARLY DAYS ARE STILL RELATIVELY AVAILABLE IN THE WILD, BUT ABUNDANT (IF SOMEWHAT MORE COSTLY) AT THE SUPERMARKET.

SO COOK, AND EXPERIMENT AND PERHAPS LEARN A LITTLE ABOUT NATIVE NEW ENGLAND COOKING. WE'LL TAKE A LITTLE FROM HERE AND A LITTLE FROM THERE AND HAVE SOME FUN.

THE AMERICAN SALMON ARE LARGER THAN THOSE IN EUROPE. THEY WERE ONCE AS PLENTIFUL AS CODFISH IN THE MAJOR RIVERS OF THE NORTHEAST.

AFTER MANY SUCCESSFUL SEASONS, THE INDIANS KNEW THE EXACT TIME OF YEAR THE SALMON WOULD SPAWN. WHEN THIS "RUN" UP THE RIVERS BEGAN, THE MEN AND CHILDREN WOULD GATHER ON THE BANKS TO CATCH AS MANY AS THEY COULD SO THEY MIGHT DRY AND SMOKE THEM FOR WINTER USE.

SOMETIMES THE DRIED FISH WERE POUNDED INTO A FLAT SHEET, LIKE PEMMICAN, AND STORED IN BASKETS.

THEY HAD ALL TYPES OF FISHING GEAR BUT DIP NETS WERE THE MOST COMMON, FOLLOWED BY HARPOONS AND WEIRS.

SALMON FLUFF

1 16 oz. can red salmon
3 tablespoons butter
3 tablespoons flour
1 teaspoon salt
½ teaspoon dry mustard
½ teaspoon Worchestershire
½ cup milk
½ cup cream
4 eggs, separated

Prepare 1½ hours before serving.
Preheat oven to 375°.

Butter a 1½ quart souffle dish.
In a saucepan melt butter and
stir in flour, salt, mustard and
Worchestershire until blended.
Stir in milk and cream until
thickened.

Cool a bit, then beat in egg
yolks, one at a time. Flake
salmon in a separate bowl and

7

add liquid and all to mixture.

In another bowl, beat egg
whites to stiff peaks, then
fold into mixture. Pour it
all into souffle dish and
bake 40-45 minutes. Serve
immediately. Serves 4

In the early days, there was an incredible abundance of oysters all along the Atlantic coast. The Indians merely had to wade out at low tide and gather all they needed. And they were big — six to eight inch shells were not at all uncommon.

Do avoid cooking oysters a long time, as they will toughen and lose flavor. In fact, stop cooking them the very second their edges start to curl.

GREAT OYSTER SOUP

1 quart oysters and liquor
1 cup water
1 cup white wine
1 teaspoon salt
½ teaspoon ground thyme
1 medium onion, chopped
1 teaspoon lemon peel
4 whole peppercorns
½ cup flour
¼ pound butter
1 cup heavy cream
2 anchovies, chopped
2 egg yolks
Dash each: ground cloves
             ground nutmeg
             ground mace

Put the liquor only in a saucepan and add water, ½ cup wine,
salt, thyme, onion, lemon peel,

11

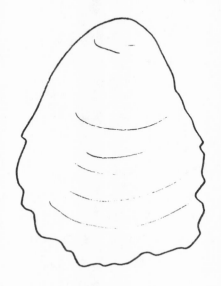

Great Oyster Soup,

cloves, nutmeg, mace and peppercorns. Heat to boiling, then simmer for 10 minutes.

Pat oysters dry and coat with flour. Heat butter in frying pan and saute oysters till golden. Add this oyster/butter mixture to simmering liquids.

Now make cream mixture with ½ cup wine, heavy cream, anchovies and egg yolks.

Add this gradually to simmering liquid and heat, but do not boil.

Serves 6

Bluefish is a nice lean fish and is still quite abundant today, especially in the waters of Long Island Sound. It is very delicious smoked and was a native favorite. The Indian captured these beauties in weirs where possible, or harpooned them from canoes.

BLUEFISH

2 pounds bluefish
Salt
Pepper
Lemon slices
Dillweed

Place the bluefish in
heavy duty aluminium
foil, enough to cover and
seal tight.

Add salt and pepper and
sprinkle with a little dillweed. Dot with butter
and place several lemon
slices on top. Seal foil
to cover and bake till
flaky (about $\frac{1}{2}$ hour at 350°).
Serves 3-4

Delicious cooked as above
on outside grill.

THE ATLANTIC WATERS OFF NEW ENGLAND WERE TEEMING WITH FISH AND SHELLFISH WHEN THE PILGRIMS LANDED. AMONG THE EDIBLE FISH WERE BLACK FISH, TURBOT, HERRING, HADDOCK, EELS, CRABS, CLAMS, OYSTERS, LOBSTER, MUSSELS AND SALMON— TO NAME JUST A FEW! THE MOST PLENTIFUL, HOWEVER, WAS THE CODFISH. DRIED COD WAS EXPORTED FROM MASSACHUSETTS IN GREAT QUANTITY AS EARLY AS 1640.

CODFISH BALLS

2 cups salt cod
4 medium potatoes
3 tablespoons butter
2 eggs
Parsley, salt and pepper
           to taste

Soak cod a half hour in water, then drain and flake it. Boil the fish with the potatoes till potatoes are done, drain and put back on heat for a minute to dry. Cool mixture $\frac{1}{2}$ hour. Mash the mixture and add butter, salt, parsley, pepper and eggs. Drop by tablespoons into DEEP hot fat and fry till golden.

Experiment with a dash of dry mustard or scallion bits, etc...

Milk, of course, was not known in New England until 1624 when the first cows were brought from England. Milk was not at all a popular drink to Indian or white man, but by-products like butter and cheese were very desirable. Since milk was not pasteurized, TB and other diseases were introduced to New England's natives with sad results.

"The" Clam Chowder

2	dozen cherrystones **or**
2	cans whole baby clams **and**
2	cans minced clams and broth
1	bottle clam juice
6-8	large potatoes, diced big
1	large onion **or** 2 medium, chopped
2	stalks celery plus leaves, chopped
3	strips bacon, cut into pieces
1	stick butter
¼	cup flour **or** cornstarch
2	cups milk, more if needed
1	cup heavy cream
1	teaspoon salt
½	teaspoon fresh ground pepper
1-2	tablespoons parsley
1	teaspoon thyme
1	teaspoon sugar

Par boil potatoes, drain. Melt butter in the pot and cook bacon, onion and celery until golden.

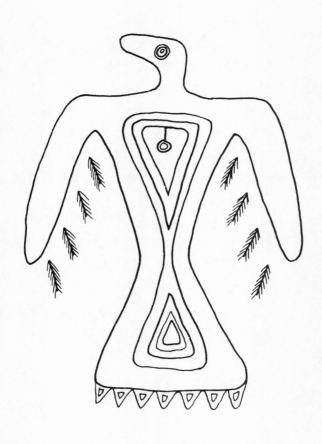

Clam Chowder - CONTINUED

Stir in flour, add potatoes, clams, broth, spices, milk, cream and simmer very slowly - Do Not Allow It To Boil!

Note: Rich and wonderful! Indian chowder was originally made with sun-flower seed oil and other nut butters.

Serves 8-12

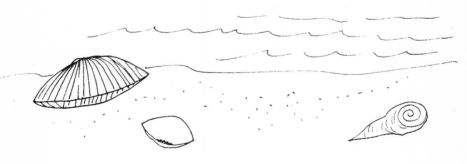

SARDINES ARE REALLY BABY HERRING. IN MAINE IT WAS INDIAN CUSTOM TO COOK THEM ON A RACK OVER AN OPEN FIRE SKEWERED ON STICKS. CHILDREN WOULD OFTEN BE SEEN GNAWING ON THEM LIKE A WALKING SNACK. IT'S A DARN SIGHT HEALTHIER THAN A LOLLYPOP, THOUGH NOT AS PRETTY.

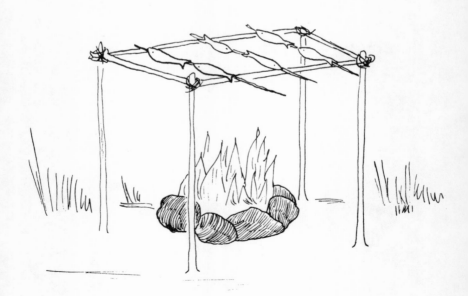

PASSAMAQUODDY SARDINES

3 cans sardines
1 cup sour creme
¼ cup vinegar
4 tbls. white wine
1 clove crushed garlic
1 teas. horseradish
½ teas. salt
¾ cup thin sliced onion
1 cup thin sliced cucumber

Make a day before serving so flavors can meld in chilling.

Drain and arrange sardines in shallow pan. Mix all other ingredients lightly and spread over sardines. Chill.

Serve on lettuce.
Serves 3-4

WHEN THE COLONISTS LANDED THEY
FOUND THAT THE INDIAN USED SHELL
MONEY AS THEIR TRADING MEDIUM.
IT WAS CALLED "WAMPUM PEAK" OR
"WAMPUM". PEAK WAS THE WHITE
PORTION OF THE SHELL; WAMPUM
WAS THE PURPLE PART AND WAS CON-
SIDERED TWICE AS VALUABLE. WAM-
PUM WAS SHAPED LIKE TUBES, EACH
PIECE ONE INCH LONG OR LESS AND
ONE EIGHTH OF AN INCH IN DIAMETER.
THEY WERE DRILLED BY HAND AND
STRUNG ON A STRING WHICH WAS
MEASURED IN "CUBITS", THE DISTANCE
FROM THE TIP OF THE LITTLE FINGER
TO THE ELBOW, REGARDLESS OF THE
SIZE OF A PERSON.

SHELLS WERE USED IN OTHER
WAYS BY THE PEOPLES OF THE
EASTERN WOODLANDS. THEY WERE
USED AS DIGGING TOOLS AND GIANT
SCALLOP SHELLS (SIX TO SEVEN
INCHES WIDE) WERE OFTEN USED
AS DISHES.

CLAM CAKES

1 can minced clams
                    and juice
1½ cups flour
1 teaspoon baking powder
1 egg white
Pinch each: salt, pepper, sugar

Mix together and drop by tablespoons into VERY hot oil (at least 1").

Cook 'till golden. It only takes a couple of minutes, so don't go away!

Drain and devour. You may want to sprinkle more salt on them.

Serves 4

25

HARD AS IT IS TO BELIEVE, LOBSTERS WERE <u>VERY</u> PLENTIFUL WHEN THE PILGRIMS ARRIVED AND THEY CAME IN GREAT SIZE — FIVE TO TEN POUNDS.

THEY WERE EASY ENOUGH TO GATHER JUST BY PICKING THEM UP SINCE THEY LIKED SALT-WATER POOLS ALONG THE SHORELINE. THE INDIAN COOKED THEM THE SAME WAY THEY COOKED CLAMS, IN PITS WITH SEAWEED AND HOT ROCKS.

LOBSTER SALAD

$\frac{1}{2}$ pound cooked lobster meat
2 tablespoons mayonnaise
1 stalk celery, diced
$\frac{1}{2}$ small onion or scallion, diced
1 teaspoon paprika
Salt to taste

Mix all together — Chill.
Serve in toasted and buttered
hot dog rolls.   Serves 2

Iroquois Soup

```
1      pound fish
1/2    pound sliced mushrooms
2      quarts water
4      packages beef boullion
2      tablespoons cornmeal
1      large onion, chopped
1 1/2  cups dried lima beans
1      clove garlic, minced
1      tablespoon parsley
1-2    tablespoons butter
       dash basil
       dash fresh ground pepper
       salt to taste.
```

Soak limas overnight. Next day: sauté minced garlic, onion and fish in butter, stirring frequently to break fish into pieces (about 5 mins).

CONTINUED

THE IROQUOIS FALSE FACE SOCIETY
WAS A GROUP OF MEN WHO WORE
STRANGE, GROTESQUE OR HUMOROUS
WOODEN MASKS TO RID THEIR PEOPLE
OF EVIL SPIRITS AND THEIR
INFLUENCE.

THE IROQUOIS WERE A VERY RELIGIOUS
PEOPLE, BELIEVING IN MANY SPIRITS;
THEY ALSO PLACED GREAT VALUE ON
THEIR DREAMS. THE MAJOR CEREMONY
OF THE FALSE FACES WAS IN MID-
WINTER WHEN THINGS WERE PARTICULARLY
BLEAK. THE CEREMONY, CALLED THE
"MASTER OF LIFE", WAS HELD TO WIN
BACK THE GREEN GROWTH OF SPRING AND
THE GOODNESS OF LIFE FROM THE EVIL
SPIRIT OF WINTER.

Iroquois Soup, 'CONTINUED

Then add water, boullion,
mushrooms, parsley, basil,
pepper, cornmeal, salt and
drained limas.

Cook until beans are soft,
about 30-40 minutes.
Serves 4-6.

IROQUOIS
WOODEN
MASK

31

Rich Oyster Dressing

For turkey 14-20 pounds
or baked alone in foil

6 cups bread cubed
1 cup celery, chopped
1 tablespoon minced parsley
2 tablespoons chopped onion
2 teaspoons salt
½ teaspoon pepper
1 cup melted butter
2 cups chopped oysters

Mix together and stuff lightly.

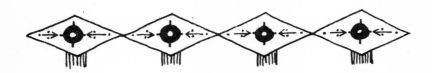

MOST EARLY COLONIAL SETTLE-
MENTS WERE EITHER ON OR
NEAR THE SHORELINE; THIS WAS
ALSO TRUE FOR INDIAN COMMUNI-
TIES AND BOTH CULTURES ATE
A GREAT DEAL OF SEAFOOD.

BEFORE THE WHITE MAN, FISH
WERE SPEARED, HOOKED, NETTED
AND TRAPPED IN QUANTITY. SIXTY
YEARS AGO, A HUGE FISH TRAP,
ALMOST 4500 YEARS OLD, WAS
DISCOVERED NEAR BOSTON. THE
TRAP COVERED AN AREA OF MORE
THAN TWO ACRES. IT WAS AN
IMPORTANT DISCOVERY BECAUSE
IT INDICATES THAT THERE WAS A
VERY LARGE, ORGANIZED INDIAN
COMMUNITY SETTLED THERE AT
THAT TIME.

Fish Stock

3   carrots
3   stalks celery
2   onions
1   bunch parsley
2   cups white wine
3   bay leaves
½   teaspoon thyme
2   pounds of fish (you can include head and bones)

In a large pot, add all of the above with enough water to cover. Simmer 1-2 hours. Strain and freeze in usable quantities. Use for chowders, soups, and delicate sauces.

left: <u>LITTLENECK</u> CLAM
RAW ON THE HALF-SHELL
ACTUALLY A SMALL QUAHOG
HARD SHELL

left: <u>CHERRYSTONE</u> CLAM
RAW ON THE HALF-SHELL OR IN
RECIPES. ALSO A QUAHOG
BUT LARGER THAN A
LITTLENECK. HARD SHELL

right: <u>STEAMER</u> CLAM
STEAMED FOR CLAMBAKES
ALSO FOR FRYING
SOFT SHELL

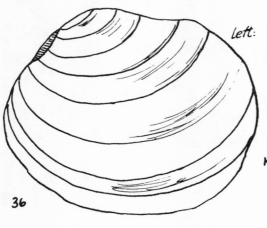

left: <u>QUAHOG</u> CLAM
BEST FOR CHOWDERS
UNDER 4 INCHES. OVER
4" IT IS CALLED "SEA-
CLAM" AND VERY TOUGH.
HARD-SHELL
KNOWN AS WAMPUM CLAM

36

A CLAMBAKE

An Indian clambake can be a great experience, try this one for 12. If you really want to splurge and make a whole day out of it, have a keg of beer, some clams on the half shell (3 dozen), some cold shrimp (3 dozen) and a huge green salad.

a bushel of steamer clams
a dozen lobsters
a dozen baking potatoes
2 dozen ears of corn

Early in the day, dig a pit three feet wide and about two and a half feet deep. Line the pit half way up with rocks (do not use slate as it splits or explodes) and build a substantial wood fire on top of them. Keep it

SIDE VIEW OF THE PIT:

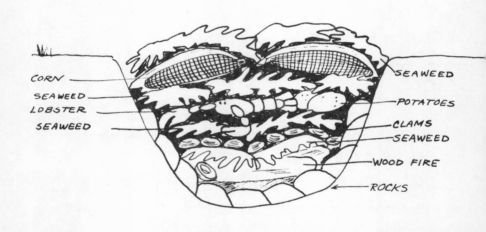

CORN

SEAWEED

LOBSTER

SEAWEED

SEAWEED

POTATOES

CLAMS

SEAWEED

WOOD FIRE

ROCKS

going about two or three hours, so that the rocks get really hot.

Fill a large bucket with seawater and lots of seaweed to keep ready by the pit. When you feel the rocks are really hot, put a layer of wet seaweed on them, then a layer of clams, another layer of seaweed, then the lobsters and potatoes, more seaweed, then the corn (leave husks on, but remove the silk), top it off with more seaweed.

Let everything steam, cook, bake, whatever, for 30 minutes. Meanwhile, melt $1\frac{1}{2}$ pounds of butter for dipping the clams and lobster. The other half pound of butter is for the corn and potatoes.

After you have a wonderful time, don't forget to fill the pit up.

Thanksgiving

There are many versions of the first Thanksgiving and what was served, but it is generally agreed that the Great Sachem Massassoit attended with about ninety of his men and that there was a great feast. Some accounts say the feasting lasted three days, others refer to it as a breakfast, and still more say an all day feasting occurred.

According to tradition, they had deer and "wild fowle" (including, of course, wild turkey), fish, corn and beans. Even so, it was hardly a gourmet's delight since the colonists were living pretty close to the bone that first winter, and the combined cooking techniques of the colonists and the Indians had yet to come to full flower.

EACH SUCCEEDING YEAR AS HARVEST HOME (THANKSGIVING) APPROACHED, THERE WAS ELABORATE PREPARATION TO MAKE IT A TRULY GRAND OCCASSION. WITH EACH HARVEST CAME MORE PLENTY, AND BY THE MIDDLE OF THE EIGHTEENTH CENTURY IT REACHED IT'S APEX. A TYPICAL TRADITIONAL MENU OF THAT PERIOD:

OYSTER STEW
ROAST TURKEY WITH CORNBREAD AND SAUSAGE STUFFING
MASHED BUTTERNUT AND TURNIP
PEAS AND CREAMED ONIONS
CANDIED SWEET POTATOES
MASHED POTATOES
CRANBERRY SAUCE AND APPLESAUCE
CHUTNEYS AND GRAVIES
PLUM PUDDING AND INDIAN PUDDING
PUMPKIN, MINCE AND APPLE PIES
CHEESES AND FRUIT
WINES AND CIDERS

WILD TURKEYS WERE FOUND IN
GREAT NUMBERS WHEN THE WHITE
MAN LANDED AND WEIGHED AS
MUCH AS FIFTY POUNDS. SINCE
THEY WERE A LITTLE TOUGHER
THAN TODAY'S VARIETIES, THEY
WERE USUALLY COOKED ON A
SPIT OVER A FIRE FOR A LONG
PERIOD OF TIME. STEWING
THEM FOR HOURS WAS ANOTHER
METHOD OF TENDERIZING THEM.
BECAUSE OF THEIR SIZE, MANY
MEALS WERE MADE FROM JUST ONE
OF THESE BIRDS, AND CONSEQUENTLY
THERE ARE HUNDREDS OF RECIPES
FOR USING LEFTOVER TURKEY MEAT.

TURKEY WAS ONE OF THE MOST EX-
CITING NEW EXPORTS TO EUROPE
FROM THE NEW WORLD. THEY WERE
FIRST BROUGHT BACK TO EUROPE
BY EXPLORERS IN THE 16TH
CENTURY.

SCALLOP OF TURKEY

2 cups sliced or cubed cooked
                    turkey
4 cooked potatoes, sliced
1 cup grated cheese (cheddar,
                    swiss, etc.)
½ onion, chopped fine
2 tablespoons sherry
1 can cream of celery soup

Butter a baking dish and layer it with potatoes and turkey. Sprinkle onion and grated cheese over it.

Mix soup with ⅓ can of water and the sherry and pour over dish. Bake covered 40 minutes at 350°.

Serves 4

43

FRICASSEE OF CHICKEN

4 large chicken breasts
½ pound butter
½ cup white wine or sherry
½ cup milk or cream
Flour, Salt, Pepper and Mace

Dust chicken with flour, mace, salt and pepper. Melt 1½ sticks of butter in large skillet and saute' chicken for 1 hour (½ hour each side). Remove chicken. Pour ½ cup of wine into pan and let alcohol cook away. Add remaining butter, cream and enough flour to make a nice gravy. Serves 4.

THE DUCK DECOY WAS AN INVENTION
OF THE NATIVE AMERICAN. THEY
WERE MADE OF REED, SEWN TO-
GETHER WITH A FIBER THREAD AND
COVERED WITH FEATHERS.

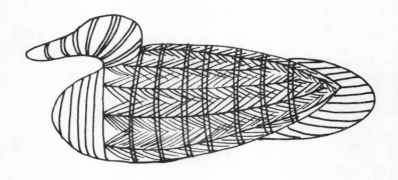

TO KEEP DUCK FROM SPATTERING
TOO MUCH, PRICK THE SKIN AND
USE ONLY WARM BASTING LIQUID
(TRY WARM CIDER). SAVE THE
DUCK FAT — IT IS WONDERFUL TO
BRAISE POTATOES AND CARROTS.
BE SURE TO ADD A LITTLE BROWN
SUGAR IF YOU DO THIS.

"Wild + Wonderful" Duck

Stuff a 4-5 pound duck with:

2   apples, cut up
2   oranges, peeled and cut up
1   cup cubed bread
1   small onion, chopped
1   stalk celery, chopped
1   tablespoon raisins
1   egg
1   tablespoon butter
1   teaspoon sugar
Salt, pepper and poultry
seasoning to taste

Mix the above in a bowl, then stuff and roast as follows:

30 mins. @ 375°, then
1 hour @ 250°, then
30 mins. @ 400°

THERE WERE UNLIMITED
AMOUNTS OF GAME BIRDS
IN THE EASTERN WOODLANDS
WHEN THE COLONISTS ARRIVED
INCLUDING PARTRIDGE, GROUSE,
WILD DUCK, PHEASANT, QUAIL
AND WILD TURKEY.

SOME COMMON NATIVE
STUFFINGS :

> CURRANTS
> WILD GRAPES
> CHESTNUTS
> HAZELNUTS

PHEASANT WITH CHESTNUT STUFFING

Stuffing:

Roast 2 pounds chestnuts, cool and peel. Grate in blender or in processor. Add 2 tablespoons bread crumbs, 1 small grated onion, 1 stalk celery, 1 tablespoon brandy (or sherry) and process a few seconds.

Stuff two 3-pound pheasants. Rub the birds outside with salt, pepper and ground rosemary. Cover the breasts with strips of bacon.

Roast at 450° for 15 minutes, then at 325° for 30-40 mins. Serve with chutney.

Serves 2-3

49

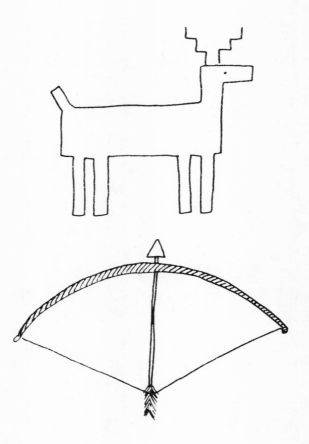

ROAST VENISON

Venison should always be tender-
ized in a marinade of some
sort as it tends to be tough. This
recipe is for approximately 5 lbs. of
meat.

Marinade: 2 cups wine
　　　　　　　(Red, White, even Sherry)
　　　　　2 tablespoons oil
　　　　　1 medium onion, sliced
　　　　　1 clove garlic, minced
　　　　　2 large bay leaves
　　　　　1 sprig thyme
　　　　　1 sprig savory
　　　　Salt and pepper to taste

Heat marinade to blend the
flavors, cool and then pour over
meat. Cover and refrigerate at
least 12 hours (2 days is even
better). Turn meat occasionally
to wet all surfaces. Roast at
325°　25-35 mins. per pound.
Serves 4-6

THIS ORIGINAL DISH REALLY
EVOLVED OVER SEVERAL SUMMER
MONTHS WHEN I WAS COOKING
OUTSIDE A LOT AND TRYING TO
ELABORATE ON CHILI AND
SUCCOTASH.

IT IS A GREAT MEAL THAT
CAN BE DIFFERENT EVERY TIME.
EXPERIMENT WITH LEFT-OVERS.

INDIAN VEGETABLES

4	strips bacon
2	large onions, sliced
3	cups sliced green and yellow summer squash
1	cup cubed eggplant
1	cup green beans
1	cup whole baby carrots
1	bell pepper, sliced
1/2	pound mushrooms
1	can tomato sauce
1	large can red kidney beans
1	large can chick peas
1	pound meat (ground beef, pork, sweet sausage, steak or a combination of any and all)
1/2	cup rice, preferably wild
1/4	cup molasses

Serves 12

This dish is best cooked outside over an open fire in a very large skillet, but it can be just as successful cooked

Indian Vegetables-

inside on your stove. You can vary the recipe each time by using what you have available. The only vegetable I would not recommend is beets. Some vegetables should be par-boiled. Corn is a great addition.

Saute' bacon, remove and save. Saute' onions in the bacon fat, add pepper, mushrooms, other vegetables and meat and cook for 5 mins. Before adding rest of ingredients, season with parsley, garlic salt, sage, marjoram, thyme, and chili powder. Now add balance of ingredients and saute' about 15 minutes.

Delicious served with green salad, corn bread and applesauce, Indian style.

CHICKEN CORN CHOWDER

2	chickens, split
4	cans creamed corn
4	sticks celery
2	onions, chopped
4	carrots, cut in pieces
6	potatoes, cut in pieces
1	cup flour
1	egg
2	tablespoons butter
1	cup cream
$\frac{1}{2}$	teaspoon each: salt, cayenne, sage, parsley, thyme and basil

Put chickens, celery, onions, carrots, spices and potatoes in a large pot and cover with water. When the chicken is tender, remove from broth and skin, debone and cut into bite-size pieces - return to broth. Now add corn. In a small bowl mix flour, cream (or milk) and egg, then add this slowly to the chowder. Simmer another ten minutes until thickened. Add butter, stir to melt, serve hot. Serves 8-10.

"SUCCOTASH" IS AN INDIAN WORD WHICH MEANS ANY DISH CONTAINING BOTH CORN AND BEANS. NEW ENGLAND SUCCOTASH USUALLY CONTAINED MEAT AND FOWL; CORNED BEEF AND CHICKEN WERE POPULAR AS WAS WILD TURKEY LEFT-OVERS.

TRUE SUCCOTASH IS A FAR CRY FROM THE CORN AND LIMA BEAN CANS OFFERED UNDER THE SAME NAME IN THE SUPERMARKETS. THIS FORM OF SUCCOTASH ORIGINATED AND IS VERY POPULAR IN THE SOUTH.

Succotash

4 cups baked beans
1 can whole kernal corn
1 can lima beans
3 cooked potatoes, cut up
½ pound corned beef, cooked
½ pound chicken, cooked
1 can stewed tomatoes (OPTIONAL)
Salt and pepper to taste

Put all above in a Dutch oven or large skillet. Be sure to include the liquid of the canned ingredients and cut up the meat. You may substitute any leftover meat— pork or sausage is very good. Cook over medium heat about 10-12 minutes.   Serves 4-6

You might want to refrigerate or freeze some or all of this dish. It is one of those things that is maybe even better the second time it is heated, like many stews and chowders.

Salad of Wild Greens

Watercress
Dandelion greens and crowns
Day lily buds, unopened
Scallion tops

Dressing: ¼ cup cider vinegar
1 teaspoon sugar
1 teaspoon salt
Pinch dill, basil
Fresh ground pepper
¼ cup oil
(preferably sesame oil)

Mix together and toss over greens, lightly.

Watercress is an abundant wild food in America and can be found in most streams.

One method I have used successfully is to root watercress from the supermarket in a glass and put it in a stream (or even a trickle, as we had) of water. It roots readily and can be harvested for many years.

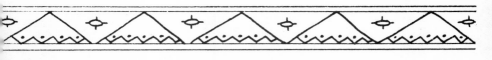

WATERCRESS SALAD

1 bunch watercress
¼ pound raw spinach
Several raw mushrooms - sliced
Slices of red onion
Few chunks swiss, cheddar and
                blue cheese
Bacon, crumbled on top

Dressing: ½ teaspoon sugar
              salt, pepper, dill weed
              cider vinegar
              salad oil

    or:

              juice of 1 lemon
              ½ teaspoon sugar
              salt, pepper (light on salt!)
              olive oil
              1-2 anchovies, cut up

Mix ingredients, pour over
greens and toss lightly.

DILL - BEAN SALAD

1 20 oz. can white kidney beans (Cannellini)
1 teaspoon dill weed
2 stalks celery, chopped fine
1 clove garlic, minced
2 stalks scallion, sliced fine

Dressing: ⅓ cup cider vinegar
½ cup oil (more if you like)
Salt, pepper to taste

Rinse beans and combine with other ingredients. Pour dressing over and chill.

Serves 4-6

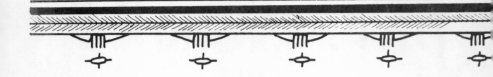

GREEN BELL PEPPERS (CAPSICUMS)
WERE NOT KNOWN IN THE EAST-
ERN WOODLANDS OF THE
NORTH, THOUGH THEY WERE
GROWN IN THE SOUTHERN
COLONIES. THEY WERE FIRST
PLANTED IN NEW ENGLAND
IN THE LATE 1600'S. PEPPERS
HAD NOT BEEN TASTED IN
EUROPE UNTIL SPANISH EXPLOR-
ERS BROUGHT THEM BACK.

ROASTED PEPPERS

Take 3 to 4 bell peppers.
Wash, quarter and place on a
skewer.

Roast over hot coals 'till
nearly black.

Season with cider vinegar,
olive oil, salt and pepper.

Very tasty with Mushroom
Soup and Squaw Bread

TWO FOODS BROUGHT BY THE
COLONISTS DURING THE SEVEN-
TEENTH CENTURY WERE COM-
BINED TO MAKE A DELICIOUS
AND POPULAR DISH FOR WHITE
MAN AND INDIAN ALIKE.

PIGS WERE INTRODUCED TO
NEW ENGLAND IN THE LATE 1600'S
ALTHOUGH PRIOR TO THAT TIME
PORK AND HAMS WERE "IMPORTED"
FROM THE SOUTH, MAINLY VIRGINIA.

APPLE TREES CAME WITH THE
FIRST SETTLERS AND BY THE
MID-EIGHTEENTH CENTURY,
APPLES WERE GROWING IN
EVERY COLONY.

APPLES & BACON

Fry 1 pound of bacon in a long handled pan over an open fire, remove bacon, set aside. Sauté 4-6 pounds of mixed varities of apples, cut in bite-sized hunks, until tender in the bacon fat. Leave skins on.

Sprinkle apples with 1 cup of brown sugar and 2 teaspoons of cinnamon. Crumble bacon on top. Stir well and serve hot.

This whole process is equally as delicious cooked on a regular stove. This is also very del-icious made with Italian sweet sausage!
Serves 6

ACORN SQUASH Baked with Apples

Par boil 2 acorn squash
(which have been split and scooped out) for 15 minutes. Then
place in a buttered baking pan.

Mix ½ cup brown sugar with 3
pared and sliced apples and add
a dash of nutmeg and cinnamon.

Fill scooped out cavities of squash
with apple mixture, dot with
butter.

Bake 40 minutes at 325°

Serves 4

PUMPKIN

Wash a small pumpkin and cut off top and remove pulp and seeds.

Put in cavity: 1 cup apple cider
½ cup honey or
brown sugar
3 tablespoons butter

Bake at 350° about 1 hour or until soft. Scoop out and serve with a little cider mixture over each portion. Serves 4

THE JERUSALEM ARTICHOKE IS
ACTUALLY A "SUNFLOWER" BULB
AND IS NATIVE TO NORTH AMERICA.
IT IS TOTALLY UNRELATED TO THE
GLOBE ARTICHOKE, WHICH IS
ACTUALLY AN EDIBLE THISTLE.

THE NATIVE AMERICAN CONSIDERED
THE JERUSALEM ARTICHOKE A HIGHLY
VALUABLE FOOD AND ACTUALLY CULT-
IVATED IT FOR CENTURIES. IT IS NO
LONGER WIDELY CULTIVATED IN THIS
COUNTRY, BUT CAN BE FOUND GROW-
ING WILD ON OLD FARM SITES.

BECAUSE OF ITS UNIQUE TASTE AND
ITS ABILITY TO BE HARVESTED ALL
WINTER, THE JERUSALEM ARTICHOKE
IS JUST NOW STARTING TO BECOME
POPULAR ONCE AGAIN. IN THE
SUPERMARKET, THEY ARE FREQUENTLY
CALLED "SUNCHOKES".

"PICKLED" JERUSALEM ARTICHOKES

Boil 2 quarts of apple cider vinegar for a few seconds and then remove from heat. Add to this mixture as it cools:

- 2 tablespoons dill weed
- 2 tablespoons celery seed
- 3 tablespoons mustard seed
- 1/4 cup honey
- 2 tablespoons dry mustard
- 1/4 cup salt
- 4 peppercorns
- 4 pieces sliced gingeroot

Scrub and slice into thin rounds 4 pounds of Jerusalem artichokes. Pack slices into clean sterilized jars and fill with cooled pickle mixture.

Marinate at least overnight.

WILD RICE IS NOT EVEN A RICE
BUT IS ACTUALLY THE SEED OF
AN AQUATIC GRASS. THE OJIBWA
(CHIPPEWA) OF THE GREAT LAKES
AREA, CALL THEMSELVES
"MENOMINEE" WHICH MEANS
"WILD RICE PEOPLE". THIS DELICIOUS
FOOD IS NATIVE TO BOTH ASIA
AND NORTH AMERICA. IT IS STILL
HARVESTED IN THE INDIAN FASHION
(USING A CANOE) IN NORTHERN
MINNESOTA, A CROP WHICH PRO-
DUCES THE MAJOR PORTION OF
THE WORLD'S SUPPLY.

HERBED WILD RICE

$\frac{1}{4}$ cup wild rice
$\frac{3}{4}$ cup white rice
Pinch parsley
Pinch basil
Pinch marjoram
Pinch sage
Pinch thyme
Salt

Cook all together slowly for
about 25 minutes in $2\frac{1}{2}$ cups
water. When done, stir in 3
tablespoons butter and serve.
Serves 4.

MUSHROOM SOUP

1 pound mushrooms, chopped
2 small sprigs of mint or basil
1 bunch scallions, sliced
2 sprigs watercress
3 tablespoons butter

Saute' above in butter just a
few minutes and add 8 cups
of water flavored by 4-5
packets of beef broth and a
little salt. Simmer 30 to 40
minutes. If you like it a little
richer, add ½ cup cream or
milk, but do not boil. Serves 6-8

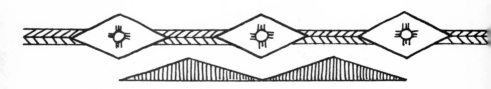

STUFFED
SQUASH

2 acorn squash, split and seeded
$\frac{1}{2}$ pound ground beef
$\frac{1}{2}$ pound ground pork (or veal)
$\frac{1}{2}$ cup uncooked oats (or bread crumbs)
$\frac{1}{4}$ cup milk
$\frac{1}{4}$ cup brown sugar
1 teaspoon salt
$\frac{1}{4}$ teaspoon mace
1 small onion, chopped

Bake squash, cut side up, for 45 minutes at 325°.

Meanwhile, in a bowl combine beef, pork (or veal), oats (or crumbs), milk, onion, mace and salt. Sauté until meat is throughly cooked. Remove squash from oven and fill cavities with meat mixture and sprinkle each half with brown sugar. Bake 15 minutes more and serve. Serves 4.

SLICED SQUASH

2 pounds any summer squash -
    zucchini, yellow or both
1 very large onion or 2 small
½ pound bacon

Cook bacon 'till done, remove and drain, leaving fat in pan. Slice onion and saute' until golden, remove. Slice and saute' squash for just a few minutes and sprinkle with parsley, basil, oregano, parmesan or cheddar cheese and a handful of bread crumbs.

Put in serving dish, cover with onions, crumble bacon on top or mush all together — it's good any way!

Serves 4

WATERCRESS IS A MEMBER OF THE MUSTARD FAMILY. THE INDIAN FOUND IT SUCCESSFUL FOR SEVERAL MEDICINAL PURPOSES. FOR EXAMPLE, IT INCREASED THE FLOW OF URINE, AS DOES FLAX AND GOLDENROD AMONG OTHERS. IT WAS ALSO BELIEVED TO EASE LABOR PAINS AND DISSOLVE GALLSTONES.

"Green"
Potato Soup

1   large onion, chopped
5   tablespoons butter
4-5   large potatoes
1½   quarts chicken broth
1   bunch watercress, chopped
2   tablespoons parsley
Pinch each: salt, pepper, nutmeg,
                        sugar
1   cup cream

Saute' the onion in 4 tablespoons of butter 'till golden.

Cube potatoes and simmer in chicken broth until soft. Add watercress, parsley, salt, pepper, nutmeg and sugar. When cooled, add the cream and 1 tablespoon butter. Keep hot, but DO NOT BOIL.

Serves 4

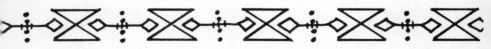

MUSTARD WAS A COMMON AND
POPULAR MEDICINAL HERB FOR
THE INDIAN ESPECIALLY IN THE
FORM OF MUSTARD PLASTERS
AND MUSTARD BATHS. IT WAS
USED FOR SORE MUSCLES, FOR
BURNS, COLDS AND FEVERS,
CHILDBIRTH AND PROSTATE
PROBLEMS.

Mustard Greens
with Bacon

In a good-size heavy pan cook 6 slices of diced bacon, remove and drain. Drain off ⅓ of the drippings and add 6 cups of chopped mustard greens and 2 or 3 tablespoons of beef broth.

Cover and cook over medium heat 15 minutes. Stir occasionally. Serves 3-4.

Variation: Cook as above, but just before serving add ½ cup grated cheese, stir to melt.   Serves 3-4

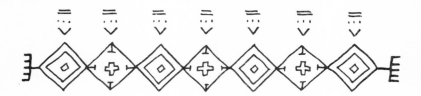

THE MALE BLOSSOM OF THE
SQUASH OR PUMPKIN IS THE
LARGEST AND SHOULD BE
PICKED JUST BEFORE IT'S
READY TO BLOOM OR DAY-
LILY BUDS CAN BE SUBSTIT-
UTED. TRY SOME SAUTEED
IN BUTTER AND ADDED TO AN
OMELET; THEY HAVE A FRESH
AND DELICATE FLAVOR. ALSO
TRY ADDING FRESH ALFALFA
SPROUTS AND SAUTEED GREEN
PEPPERS, SCALLION, MUSHROOMS
AND A DASH OF TABASCO.

BATTER DIPT
SQUASH BLOSSOMS

Picked before opening - 2 dozen male
squash blossoms

Batter: 1 cup flour
1 teaspoon cornstarch
1 teaspoon baking powder
1 egg white
Salt, pepper, parsley, ginger,
sugar to taste
Ice Water

Mix batter ingredients until blended
to the consistancy of pancake
batter and deep fry each in at
least 1" of hot oil. Serves 2-4.

Corn or maize originated in central Mexico. In the Southwest a type of corn and beans were cultivated 6000 years ago. In the Northeast, corn seems to have been around a long time too. It was cultivated in the Ohio Valley before 500 A.D. and by the Iroquois as early as 1200 A.D.

New England corn was small, only 5 inches long, with varying colors. It was planted in hills because it did not have a very strong root system. Along the coast, fish (particularly alewives) were used as a fertilizer.

CORN FRITTERS

1 large can creamed corn
2 eggs
½ cup chopped onion
¼ teaspoon salt
A little pepper
½ cup or more flour

Mix all ingredients together to the consistency of pancake batter.

Fry in HOT oil until golden. Serves 4-6

Note: Especially delicious fried in coconut oil.

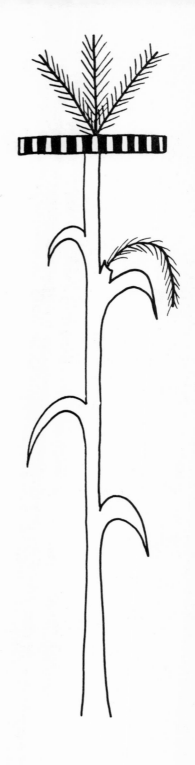

MOHAWK CORN

Saute 2 cups of whole kernal corn in 3 tablespoons of butter.

Add $\frac{1}{2}$ cup of black walnuts and $\frac{1}{2}$ teaspoon black walnut flavoring.

Heat and serve.

Serves 2.

IT IS SAID THAT POPCORN
WAS INTRODUCED TO THE WHITE
MAN AT THE FIRST THANKS-
GIVING BY MASSASOIT'S BROTHER.
IT WAS PROBABLY COOKED IN
EITHER BEAR FAT OR FISH OIL.
THE IROQUOIS ELABORATED AND
SERVED A TREAT OF POPCORN
WITH HOT MAPLE SYRUP OVER
IT; A WHITE MAN WHO TASTED
THIS TOLD HIS FRIENDS IT WAS
"CRACKERJACK."

POPCORN

Heat about ⅓ cup of oil and test by throwing in 1 kernal.

Add ⅔ cup of white popcorn.

After popping add:

    ½ cup melted sweet
                butter
    Season with herbed
    salt or sea salt

Variation: experiment with different oils —

        safflower
        sesame
        corn
        coconut
           etc...

FLOUR OF SORTS WAS MADE
BY CRUSHING WALNUTS, HAZEL-
NUTS AND ACORNS TO A POW-
DER. INDIANS USED THEM
MOSTLY AS A THICKENING AGENT.
NOT ONLY ARE NUT FLOURS
VERY NUTRITIOUS, THEY ARE
TASTY AS WELL.

Squaw Bread

To: 3 cups flour*
     1 tablespoon baking powder
     1 teaspoon salt
     1 teaspoon melted butter

Add: 1⅓ cups milk

Knead 5 minutes on a floured board and shape into
six little loaves (like ½ inch
thick hamburgers). Fry in
hot <u>bacon fat</u> 'till gold on
each side. Make sure it's
done in the middle.

Serve warm with butter,
meats, jam, etc...

*Try varied flours.

97

ASHCAKES WERE CALLED "APPONES" BY THE INDIAN. THEY WERE MADE WITH CORNMEAL AND WATER AND SHAPED INTO FLAT CAKES AND "BAKED" IN ASHES. WHEN THESE SAME CAKES WERE MADE INSIDE TO BE COOKED IN AN OVEN, THE NAME BECAME CORN PONE.

JOHNNYCAKE IS STILL ANOTHER NAME FOR THIS SAME CORNMEAL PATTIE. BOTH INDIANS AND COLONISTS TOOK IT ON TRIPS AND HUNTING, THUS THE ACTUAL NAME "JOURNEY-CAKES." TO THIS DAY, IT IS SAID THE BEST JOURNEY CAKES COME FROM RHODE ISLAND.

SINCE THE INGREDIENTS ARE SIMPLE, AND THE COOKING EASY, THEY MAKE A TERRIFIC CAMPING FOOD.

APPONES

2 cups white cornmeal
1 teaspoon salt
½ teaspoon baking soda
¼ cup oil
¾ cup boiling water
¼ cup buttermilk

Preheat oven to 350°. In a bowl, mix cornmeal, salt, baking soda and oil with a spoon 'till all ingredients are moist. Stir in boiling water, mix well and add buttermilk. Mix into soft dough.

Put ¼ cup mixture on greased cookie sheet and pat down to ½ inch thickness. Bake 35-40 minutes or until firm to the touch. Serve warm with butter and/or syrup.   Serves 2-4

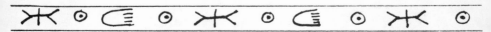

ONCE THE GREAT AMERICAN CHEST-
NUT TREE PROSPERED IN THIS
COUNTRY. INDIANS ATE CHESTNUTS
FOR YEARS, USUALLY ROASTED AND
EATEN PLAIN. INDIAN WOMEN ALSO
POUNDED THEM INTO FLOUR AND
MIXED THIS WITH CORNMEAL, WRAP-
PING THE RESULT VERY TIGHTLY IN
CORN HUSKS AND THEN BOILING.

COLONISTS STORED CHESTNUTS
SUCCESSFULLY FOR WINTER USE
AND USED THEM IN MANY WAYS—
ROASTED, IN CAKES, WITH VEGETABLES,
WITH MEATS (OFTEN AS STUFFING)
AND EVEN AS DESSERTS.

Chestnut Cakes

Roast 1 pound of chestnuts, cool, peel and puree.

Add ½ small onion, chopped fine and enough cornmeal and boiling water to hold mixture together.

Make hamburger-size patties and fry in hot oil till golden on each side. Drain, salt and eat! Do not add salt before cooking as it causes cornmeal to crumble.

THERE IS AN OLD LEGEND OF THE WAY SPOON BREAD GOT IT'S NAME. IT SOUNDS LOGICAL AS MOST THINGS GET THEIR NAME IN RATHER ORDINARY FASHION.

APPARENTLY A FARMER'S WIFE MADE A CORNMEAL MUSH FOR HER HUSBAND. SHE MADE IT TOO EARLY THAT DAY, SO SHE TRIED TO KEEP IT WARM NEAR THE FIRE. HER HUSBAND WAS DELAYED AND CAME HOME VERY LATE TO FIND THAT A CRISP CRUST HAD FORMED ON THE OUTSIDE OF THE MUSH, LEAVING THE INSIDE ALL SOFT AND CREAMY. HE PICKED UP A SPOON AND ATE IT. WE HAVE CALLED IT SPOON BREAD EVER SINCE.

Spoon Bread

    5 tablespoons butter
    1 cup cornmeal
    1 teaspoon salt
    1 cup cold milk
    1 egg
    2 tablespoons brown sugar

Preheat oven to 425°. Put butter in 1½ quart baking dish in oven to melt. In mixing bowl combine corn-meal and salt. Add 2 cups boiling water and stir. Let stand to cool then stir in milk.   Add eggs and sugar and beat 'till blended. Stir in melted butter and pour into the hot baking dish.

Bake 25 minutes or 'till set. Serve with extra butter and jam.   Serves 4-6

OATMEAL BREAD

2 cups boiling water
1 cup rolled oats
½ cup molasses
2 teaspoons salt
1 tablespoon butter

Combine above ingredients and cool.
Put in another bowl:

    ½ cup lukewarm water
    1 package yeast

Dissolve yeast and add:
    4½ cups flour and
    oatmeal mixture

Beat all together and let rise until double. Add enough flour to knead (5 mins.). Shape into large round loaf and put into a greased pie plate. Let rise again and bake at 350° for 50 minutes or until it sounds hollow. Makes 1 large delicious loaf.

Pumpkin, a member of the squash family, was called "Pompion" by Native Americans. They taught the colonists to cut it into rings and hang to dry for winter food. This highly valued food is very rich in Vitamin A.

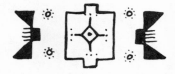

PUMPKIN BREAD

½ cup oil
1½ cup sugar
2 eggs
1 cup canned pumpkin
1¼ cup white flour
¾ cup whole wheat flour
1 teaspoon baking soda

1 teaspoon salt
¼ teaspoon baking powder
½ cup raisins
½ cup walnuts (optional)
½ teaspoon each:
   allspice, cinnamon,
   ground cloves, nutmeg

Mix sugar, oil, pumpkin, eggs and ⅓ cup water. Mix dry ingredients together, add to pumpkin mixture and stir 'till moistened. Pour into greased loaf pan and bake at 350° for an hour. Cool thoroughly. Makes 1 loaf.

Very good cold with cream cheese spread.

GINGERBREAD

2 eggs
1/2 cup sour cream
3/4 cup molasses
1/4 cup brown sugar
1 1/2 cups flour
1 teaspoon baking soda
1 1/2 teaspoon ginger
1/2 teaspoon ground clove
1/4 teaspoon salt
1/2 cup melted butter

Beat the eggs and add the sour cream, molasses and sugar and beat again. In a separate bowl sift together dry ingredients; flour, baking soda, ginger, clove and salt. Stir into sour cream mixture and add butter. Pour into greased and floured 9" square pan and bake 35 minutes at 350°.

Serve warm with whipped cream or light lemon sauce.

PRACTICALLY EVERY COOKBOOK
HAS A DIFFERENT VERSION OF
INDIAN PUDDING. ACTUALLY IT
IS NOT AN INDIAN INVENTION
AS ONE MIGHT ASSUME. THE
COLONIALS REFERRED TO CORN-
MEAL AS "INDIAN CORN" SO THEY
WOULDN'T CONFUSE IT WITH WHEAT,
HENCE THE NAME. THIS PUDDING
IS BASICALLY A CORN MUSH MADE
WITH MOLASSES, MILK AND CORN-
MEAL. LATER VERSIONS ADDED
EGGS, SUGAR, BUTTER AND SPICES.
EVEN TODAY IT IS SERVED IN
FINE RESTAURANTS THROUGHOUT
NEW ENGLAND.

INDIAN PUDDING

1½ cup raisins	1 teaspoon salt
3 cups scalded milk	½ cup sugar
1½ cups cold milk	¾ teaspoon ginger
1 cup cornmeal	¼ teaspoon nutmeg
½ cup molasses	¼ cup butter

Add raisins to hot milk. Mix cornmeal into cold milk and add slowly to hot mixture. Heat slowly 'till mixture thickens (10-15 minutes).

Now, add molasses, salt, sugar, ginger, nutmeg and butter. Pour into 2 quart baking dish and add remaining ½ cup cold milk into center of pudding. Do not stir.

Set dish in a pan of cold water (about 1"). Bake at 300° for 2½ hours. Cool 3-4 hours before serving. Serves 4-6.

BREAD PUDDING

1 loaf bread
Butter
2 eggs
Brown sugar
Raisins
Milk

Into a large bowl, tear up a loaf of sliced, buttered bread (you can mix bread varities if you wish), add eggs, a handful of brown sugar, a handful of raisins and enough milk to mix the batch to the consistency of --- yes! -- MUD. Bake 'till done (325° for about 1 hour). Serves 7-9

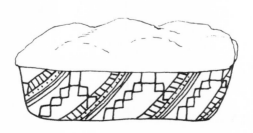

WILD BERRIES, A RICH SOURCE OF
VITAMINS A AND C FOR THE NATIVE
AMERICAN, WERE EATEN RAW AND
USED AS A MAJOR SWEETENER.
THEY, AS WELL AS THE COLONISTS,
ALSO STRUNG AND DRIED THEM FOR
WINTER USE.

IN NEW ENGLAND THE MOST COMMON
WERE:
> CRANBERRY
> BLUEBERRY
> BLACKBERRY
> RASPBERRY
> ELDERBERRY
> WILD STRAWBERRY
> HUCKLEBERRY
> GOOSEBERRY
> BLACK CURRANTS

ANY OF THESE CAN BE USED
WITH THE FOLLOWING BERRY
RECIPES.

BERRY PIE FILLING

2 tablespoons tapioca
3 pints berries
¾ cup sugar
1 tablespoon lemon juice

Mix ingredients. Using your own pie crust, prick bottom and bake at 425° for 5 minutes. Cool and fill with above mixture and cover with unbaked top crust. Brush top with milk and reduce heat to 325°. Bake 1 hour.

Here is a pie crust you might want to try: 2 cups flour, ⅔ cup shortening, 1 teaspoon salt and ¼ to ½ cup cold water. Cut in shortening, add salt and enough water to form ball. Chill ½ hour, then divide ball in two and roll out crusts on floured surface. Bake as above.

GRUNTS AND SLUMPS WERE EARLY DESSERTS MADE OF FRUITS AND DUMPLINGS. THE SOUND OF THE BERRIES COOKING PROVOKED THE NAME "GRUNT" IN MASSACHUSETTS (THEY ALWAYS LIKE TO BE A LITTLE DIFFERENT).

IN VERMONT, RHODE ISLAND AND MAINE A GRUNT WAS CALLED "SLUMP."

BOYSENBERRY SLUMP

Berry Mixture: 2 cups berries
                  1 cup water
                  $\frac{1}{2}$ cup sugar
        Mix and bring to a boil.

Dumplings: 1 cup flour
                  1 teaspoon salt
                  3 large teaspoon
                     baking powder
                  $\frac{1}{2}$ cup milk
                  3 shakes pepper

Sift flour, baking powder and
salt, stir to mix. Add milk
slowly and mix to a heavy
wet dough. Add pepper.

Drop by tablespoons into
berry mixture. Cover and
DO NOT RAISE LID for 15
minutes over medium-low heat.
Serve warm with cream.
Serves 4.

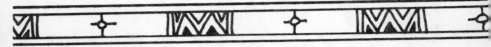

ONE OF THE MOST IMPORTANT
GIFTS THE WHITE MAN GAVE
THE INDIAN WAS THE APPLE.
APPLE TREES WERE GROWN
IN INDIAN GARDENS AND PRO-
VIDED YET ANOTHER WINTER
STAPLE WHICH COULD BE
DRIED AND STORED. FOR
THE INDIAN, THE APPLE PRO-
VIDED FOOD, DRINK (CIDER AND
HARD CIDER), AND A PRESERVATIVE
(VINEGAR).

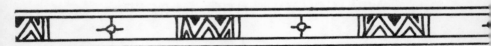

APPLESAUCE

Wash and core any amount of apples. Remove skin from half. Cook over low heat with just enough water to keep from burning.

A little piece of lemon is nice, but not essential.

When soft, add $\frac{1}{2}$ cup of sugar (brown preferred) for every three cups of apples. Touch of cinnamon and salt, if you like.

"SASSAMANESH" IS THE NATIVE WORD FOR CRANBERRY AND THIS MARSH-GROWN FRUIT WAS USED NOT ONLY FOR FOOD, BUT FOR MEDICINE AND DYE AS WELL. MEDICINALLY, IT WAS USED TO TREAT BLADDER DISORDERS AMONG INDIANS; THE COLONISTS USED IT TO TREAT SCURVY ON LONG VOYAGES AS IT HAS GREAT KEEPING QUALITY.

IN OCTOBER, THE GAY HEADERS, MEMBERS OF THE WAMPANOAG CONFEDERATION ON MARTHA'S VINEYARD, CELEBRATE CRANBERRY DAY. THE CHILDREN PICK CRAN-BERRIES AND PICNIC AND GATHER TO HEAR STORIES WHICH RENEW THEIR HERITAGE.

CRANBERRY RELISH

1 quart cranberries
1 cup water
1 cup brown sugar
2 apples, peeled + chopped
2 oranges, peeled + chopped
3 tbls. grated orange peel
1 cup walnuts, chopped

COOK CRANBERRIES IN WATER 10 MINS. OVER MEDIUM HEAT. ADD ALL OTHER INGREDIENTS EXCEPT NUTS AND COOK TILL MIXTURE THICKENS, STIRRING FREQUENTLY.

REMOVE FROM HEAT + ADD NUTS. WHEN COOL, PUT INTO 3 STERILIZED PINT JARS, COVER + REFRIGERATE.
Makes 3 pints.

It is the seeds of the mustard plant which are used to make yellow mustards. Gather as many seeds as you can and try grinding them in a food processor to a fine powder. Store in a clean dry jar and use in any recipe that calls for dry mustard. Try adding a pinch to egg salad or baked beans.

HOT MUSTARD

Makes 2 cups.

     1 cup dry mustard
     1 cup white wine vinegar
     1 cup brown sugar
     2 eggs
     1 teaspoon salt

Blend all ingredients in processor (or bowl) and cook in double-boiler top 'till thickened. Cool and put into sterilized jars. Refrigerate.

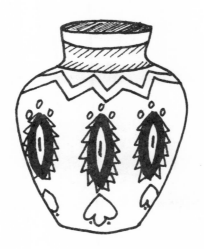

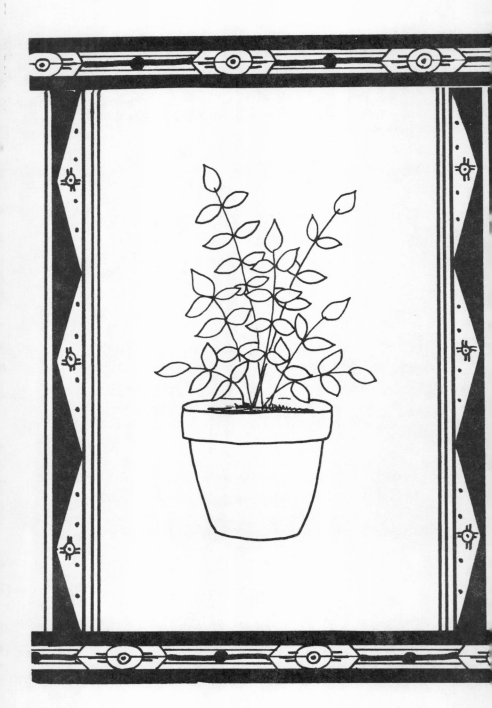

MINT VINEGAR

2 cups mint leaves
1 cup brown sugar
1 quart cider vinegar

Wash mint leaves. Boil sugar and vinegar together and add mint leaves.

Bring to boil again and simmer for 5 minutes. Strain and bottle in sterile bottles. Cork tightly.

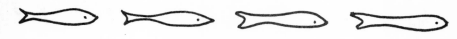

SAUCES FOR FISH

TARTAR:
- ½ cup mayonnaise
- 2 tablespoons minced sweet pickles
- 1 tablespoon parsley
- 1½ tablespoons lemon juice
- 1 tablespoon minced onion or scallion

Mix together, cover + chill.

HORSERADISH:
- ½ cup mayonnaise
- ¼ cup minced dill pickle
- 1½ tablespoons horse-radish
- 1 tablespoon cream or milk
- dash pepper
- dash dillweed

Mix together, cover + chill.

ALGONQUIN
CLAY VESSEL

CHIPPEWA (OJIBWAY)
BIRCH BARK VESSEL

IROQUOIS
CLAY VESSEL

128

BEVERAGES + TEAS

Indians used some of the following as a base for their beverages.

BIRCH

BLACKBERRY

CHAMOMILE

CHICKORY

DANDELION

DILL

ELDERBERRY

GOLDEN ROD

MAPLE

MINT

SASSAFRAS

APPLES AS WE KNOW THEM ARE NOT
NATIVE TO NORTH AMERICA, ALTHOUGH A
TYPE OF CRABAPPLE DID EXIST BEFORE
THE WHITE MAN. THE FRUIT WAS NOT
REALLY EDIBLE AND THERE IS NO RECORD
OF INDIAN USAGE.

CIDER BECAME A STAPLE DRINK, PERHAPS
THE STAPLE DRINK, IN NEW ENGLAND
ABOUT 1638 WHEN THE SAPLINGS BROUGHT
BY THE PILGRIMS FINALLY ESTABLISHED
THEMSELVES. HARD CIDER WAS SOMETIMES
MIXED WITH RUM TO MAKE A DRINK CALLED
"STONEWALL". I WONDER IF THAT IS WHERE
THE TERM "STONED" CAME FROM?

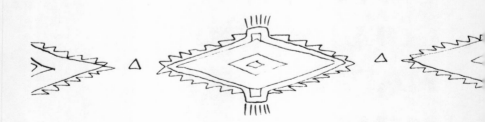

MULLED CIDER

Put 1 gallon apple cider and 1 cup of brown sugar in a huge pot, add a cheesecloth bag filled with:

- 10 whole cloves
- 10 whole allspice
- 5 sticks cinnamon
    (broken in pieces)

Set on wood stove (or regular stove on low-simmer) for at least 1 hr. Before serving, remove bag and float lemons sliced on top. Serve warm in mugs. Serves 16-20

Variation: If you want to eliminate the allspice, stick 20 cloves in an orange and let it float. Use 5 cinnamon sticks, but do not break.

For special "flavoring" add 1 pint dark rum.

DANDELION WINE

4 qts. dandelion blossoms
4 qts. boiling water
4 oranges
4 lemons
2 envelopes yeast
5 lbs. sugar

Wash blossoms and put in a huge pickle crock (any large crock will do). Pour boiling water over blossoms. Cover for two days.

On the third day, strain and put liquid only back in crock. Add the oranges and lemons (sliced and seeded). Add the yeast (dissolved in $\frac{1}{2}$ cup warm water) and the sugar. Stir and cover for three full days. Then strain out fruit and pour into sterilized bottles with light corks. Keep in cool place 1 month. Makes 5-6 qts.

ELDERBERRY WINE

4   quarts elderberries
4   quarts of water
3   pounds of sugar
½   cup lemon juice
1   package yeast

Take all stems from berries
and simmer berries in water
about 15 minutes. Strain
liquid into enamel pan or a
crock.   Add sugar and lemon
juice and when it has cooled a bit, add the yeast. Put
away to work the fermenting
process for 2 or 3 months.
Bottle when clear. Makes
4 quarts.

WHITE SUMAC BERRIES ARE
POISONOUS.

THE CRIMSON BERRIES OF
CONE SHAPE HAVE A REFRESH-
ING TASTE AND WERE MADE
INTO A COOLING DRINK BY
INDIANS. SUMAC IS HIGH IN
MALIC ACID, LIKE APPLES.
MIXED WITH APPLES, IT MAKES
A TERRIFIC JELLY BECAUSE
IT SETS SO QUICKLY.

TO MAKE SUMAC JUICE, USE
THE RED CONES AND COVER
THEM WITH WATER. BOIL FOR
10 MINS, MASHING FREQUENTLY,
THEN STRAIN OFF LIQUID.

SUMAC-ADE

Boil 3 cups of sumac juice for 3 mins. with 2 cups of sugar.

Keep this syrup refrigerated and add two tablespoons to water, club soda, tonic, lemonade, etc... for a cooling drink.

THE NATIVE AMERICAN GATHERED
MAPLE TREE SAP AND DEVELOPED
THE PROCESS OF MAKING IT INTO
SYRUP LONG BEFORE THE PILGRIMS
CAME. THE COLONISTS BROUGHT
IRON POTS WHICH HELPED EASE
THE TASK OF BOILING THE SAP
DOWN. SINCE SUGAR AND
MOLASSES HAD TO BE IMPORTED,
MAPLE SUGAR OR MAPLE SYRUP
IS CALLED FOR IN MOST OLD
NEW ENGLAND RECIPES.

UNTIL THE MIDDLE OF THE
NINETEENTH CENTURY, MAPLE
SUGAR WAS MUCH CHEAPER
THAN WHITE SUGAR. TODAY,
A MERE QUART OF MAPLE
SYRUP COSTS ABOUT SEVEN
DOLLARS.

MAPLE BEER

2 cups dark rum
1 pt. dark heavy maple syrup
1 gal. water
2 tbls. lemon juice
1 cup freshly made tea
1 pkg. yeast

Add rum to water, stir.
Mix in lemon juice, tea
and yeast.

Put in crock for 3 days.
Bottle and refrigerate.
Makes 4 quarts.

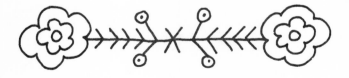